The Power Codes

The Language and Habits of the
Most Powerful People on the Planet

Stephanie Jupiter

Order this book online at www.trafford.com
or email orders@trafford.com

Most Trafford titles are also available at major online book retailers.

Printed in the United States of America.

ISBN: 978-1-4269-7574-5 (sc)

Trafford rev. 08/04/2011

 www.trafford.com

North America & international
toll-free: 1 888 232 4444 (USA & Canada)
phone: 250 383 6864 ♦ fax: 812 355 4082

Written by Stephanie Jupiter
Founder of the
Science of Life University

Developmental Tools for a Strong Mind, Body and Soul
www.soluniversity.com

This Book is dedicated to the manifestation of World Peace now. Thank you to all human beings who have and are actively working to bring about world peace. You are my heroes and I love you much. A special thanks to my mother, father, daughters and brother, who always support me with 100% love unconditionally.

Table of Content

Introduction xi

Pre-Test..1

Yes, You Can!..3

What Will it Take? 9

Power Code One - With the Power of Self Love,
All things are Possible 13

Power Code Two - Powerful People are Patient 19

Power Code Three - Powerful People are Honest..................24

Transition...31

Power Code Four - Powerful People are Fair.........................33

Power Code Five - Powerful People are Responsible 38

Power Code Six - Powerful People are Attentive 41

Power Code Seven - Powerful People are Open to
Learning (Accepting) 46

Power Code Eight - Powerful People are Powerful 53

Power Code Nine - Powerful People are Loyal 59

Power Code Ten - Powerful People are United 65

The Power Code Reminders and Quick Steps.......................68

A P.S. Message about Self Love 70

Self Love and Beyond 71

Love 360 Vocabulary Glossary 72

End of Course Exam 74

The goal of the information contained in this book is to assist you with making the ultimate shift. Any human being who is unaware of their unique purpose, role and responsibilities for being on this planet earth is in need of a major alignment. This shift is not about what someone else is doing or not doing in your life this shift is about discovering what are you naturally designed to do and doing it. This book is called the power codes because the ultimate shift is all about remembering the codes also known as a language that gives you access to every resource you need to fulfill you.

"People are not poor because they lack programs and services; people are poor because they lack power."
   Jim Dunn, Peoples Institute for Survival and Beyond

Based on the wisdom in Mr. Dunn's quote, the most important question to ask at ourselves at this junction of our collective human being experience is not who am I. The most important question to ask ourselves is what is Power?

Understanding what genuine Power is opens the door to every human beings ultimate shift.

The Power Codes awakens the knowledge of self that the majority of human beings have been distracted from due to a dogged pursuit of an artificial dream. This artificial dream is brought on and fueled by an artificial intelligence virus (A.I. V.).

Commit to making the ultimate shift, crack the power codes inside and gain the instant peace of mind that only a knowledge of self can give you access to.

There is a simple universal formula for happiness by which all human beings live:

Getting what your heart desires = Happiness
Not Getting what your heart desires = Unhappiness

Sustained happiness is peace of mind. Genuine happiness is a rare occurrence in today's time because there is an essential ingredient in happiness that many people tend to overlook. In the pursuit for happiness many people forget to fully embrace their hearts desires.

"When what we are is what we want to be, that's happiness."
Malcolm S. Forbes

The formula for happiness is so simple. However, without the essential ingredient it has become one the most difficult experiences to achieve in a lifetime.

Genuinely happy people are powerful people who are at peace with themselves and truly understand the nature of focusing only on what they desire to experience. Happy people also understand how this behavior affects every relationship in which they are involved. The Most Powerful People on this planet are those who have taken full ownership of their life and are creating the life they truly desire to experience.

The ten universal lessons in this book are designed to reconnect you with your inner source of power. You will find yourself on a mental journey that fully engages your attention toward a greater love for self. Your attitude will change from one of denial, in which you ignore or put off your personal desires, to an attitude of fulfillment, in which you recognize and consistently pursue what you truly desire to experience.

Your language will evolve from I can't – to I can – to I will – to I am – which is the final phase. In the **I am** phase, you will discover the greatest secret of the Power codes. Let us discover this precious secret together and awaken a greater love for our lives.

Test Yourself

Here is a quick test you can use to check yourself for the artificial intelligence virus (AIV) infection which is the main culprit that interferes with and distracts you from your power.

> 1. What is your unique purpose for being on this planet earth?

If your answer to question one is not crystal clear to you then you are infected. Colleagues and I at the Relationship Fitness Center have researched and studied how to rid ourselves of AIV for over the past 20 years and now I share what I have personally learned with you. Just like removing a virus from your hard drive on your computer, imagine doing the same thing for your mind. Welcome to the Power Codes.

Yes, You Can!

You are truly never alone however when you develop the confidence to be willing to walk your unique path of life alone, you will then know what it really feels like to live a life of instant Peace and Power.

> "Who is there who does not want friends? First of all you are not fit to have friends until you can live without them. This is an absolute fact. The reason is this: if you are not strong enough to live alone and can only live by the aid of a friend, you are living on his or her life and not your own. So first you must stand alone, yet not alone; the infinite stands behind everything. Having demonstrated that you can stand alone and not be lonesome, then you are fit for somebody to love you. And having become this, the universal friend, the friend of all, you cannot help attracting to you all the friendships you want. You cannot help it. Having become the universal lover, that is, the embodiment of being of love, people are compelled to love you. You must attract to you all the love there is because you have learned what love is."
>
> Ernest Holmes
> Love and Law

There is a common misconception that many of us are holding on to and it is the biggest deterrent to personal growth. I do not know the exact time in history when pursuing your desire also known as selfish became such an unwanted characteristic. However for some odd reason selfishness in our society has been labeled as very unacceptable behavior. As long as we hold on to this misconception, we will remain in a state of self –doubt which breeds self-betrayal, self-neglect and self-hatred i.e. unhappiness. We must let go of this ineffective idea that our looking out for ourselves is a negative behavior. This idea affects our mental and physical health by slowing down our brain and mind computer functioning. What most people identify as selfish behavior is really stingy behavior. There is a huge difference between the two. Selfish behavior involves paying attention to your self in order to learn more about yourself so that you can evolve and effectively share yourself with others. Stingy behavior is different in its intention. Stingy people will only share when they know that it will guarantee something of value in return from the other person. Stingy people do not operate from their hearts desires, stingy people operate from a position of I want to make sure I do not lose anything I have. So I will give only if I know I am going to keep what I already have and gain more. Selfish people operate from a point of having a strong desire to learn, fulfill and evolve them selves. Selfish people do not overly concern themselves with the idea of winning or losing.

Being selfish which means you are operating from a place of integrity and revealing what is truly in your heart is one of the most powerful characteristics known to mankind. When we do not do what is in our hearts, it has a deleterious affect on our overall well being. Not doing what is in your heart is the equivalent to disrespecting and hating yourself. Doing what is in your heart is the equivalent to fully loving yourself.

Is it possible to do what is in your heart all the time?
It is obvious that over 85% of our world's population does not think so.
When we do not think we can, we enter into the "I can't" phase, constantly denying the self, which is the world of impossibilities.

When we are in the world of impossibilities, we get stuck in survival mode. When we are in this mode we consistently overlook our **opportunities** to display, draw out, learn more about and develop our natural abilities and share them with others. In other words, we block the opportunity to grow to a new level of understanding of ourselves which in turn allows us to feel a greater sense of connection, purpose, love and power.

Who among us wants to feel loved and powerful? Do not deny this feeling; the alternative leads to an unwanted human condition—feeling unwanted and powerless. Be open! Have the tenacity to develop the POWER of SELF LOVE.

The Power Codes is a process that assist you with developing the power of self love so that you can awaken your full self and become one of the most powerful people on the planet.

Does Power Corrupt? Absolutely Not
By **KATE PICKERT** Tuesday, May. 20, 2008

A most intriguing article was published in Time Magazine about people who are empowered. It's opening states that: Power breeds competence, not corruption, according to a new study in the May issue of *Psychological Science*. The study, a collaboration between U.S. and Dutch researchers, finds that if people feel powerful in their roles, they may be less likely to make on-the-job errors — like administering the wrong medication to a patient.

And the article mentions further that:

> Despite the researchers' expectations, it's not entirely surprising that feeling powerless or unimportant might lead a person to take less care in his work. After all, if your efforts don't matter, why bother? Galinsky and his colleagues conducted four separate experiments with 422 volunteers, using different priming techniques and cognitive tests, and each time they got similar results. Powerful-feeling people performed better than the powerless. Galinsky says the study's conclusions could have a profound impact on social-order ideology and business. "People say the United States is a meritocracy," says Galinsky. "But let's not be too quick to say that the hierarchy that exists today is a perfect demonstration of a meritocracy — that everyone is completely ordered by their abilities — because rank in a hierarchy fundamentally alters people's basic cognitive function." The findings further support the idea, for example, that disadvantaged socioeconomic groups remain entrenched in poverty because their position puts them at a psychological disadvantage, not because they lack the ability or intelligence to succeed. In

the study's discussion, the authors suggest that the powerless in society are directed "toward a destiny of dispossession."

Please google the article and read it in its entirety. It motivated and inspired me to step up my performance in my life and I trust it will do the same for you.

What Will it Take?

A preliminary lesson about Time

Consider this. For those whom you really dislike, you would not give them the time of day. Here I am not talking about time in the sense of waiting over a long period to see things happen or change. When I say time I am talking about your immediate attention, focus and energy. This is equivalent to your time. What you pay attention to or put your energy into grows.

Let me give you a simple example of what I am talking about. One morning I went to take my shower and noticed that there was still water in the bottom of the bathtub. I looked to see if the stopper was down but the stopper was in a position which should have allowed the water to drain. I tried putting Draino into the drain, but the water still did not drain. I really did not want to call a plumber. I had too many other things to do that day and I did not want to spend the money. As I was busy getting ready for the day, my mind stayed on the bathtub issue. I could not let it rest. This was a simple, but important, issue because of the significant role the bathtub has in the house. I decided to take time out and was determined to fix it or call the plumber. For about five minutes, I tinkered with the drain and finally figured out how to unscrew the stopper and was able to look in the drain. I expected to see a lot of hair or oatmeal (that is another story) clogging the drain. But guess what I found--one of my three year olds toys completely covering up the drain pipe. Issue resolved. What a relief and a big reminder lesson on time for me.

The point of the story is that if you think something is wrong, there probably is something wrong. If the issue is important to you, then you have the intelligence to resolve it. The first step is to stop whatever else you are doing, devote time to the issue, review it to figure out what the problem is, and then fix it. Chances are it is something very simple; however, resolution will not happen unless you give it your <u>time</u>.

I know making the Ultimate Shift is not that easy for everyone. If it was, everyone would be demonstrating 100% self love all the time.

Making the Ultimate Shift requires you to:
Develop the sensitivity of a social worker;
Gain the insight of a psychologist;
Have the stamina of a marathon runner;
Have the persistence of a bulldog;
Have the self reliance of a hermit;
Have the roar of a lion;
Have the gentleness of a sheep;
Have the imagination of a renowned scientist;
Have the meditation skills of a Zen Monk;
And
Have the patience of saint.

The beauty of experiencing The Power of Self Love may not be easy but the steps are simple. They are simple because loving yourself is innate for you. This means it is natural for you to Love You.

It's OK to Love Yourself.
You were designed to Love YOU.

Love is being in rhythm with the desires of your heart.

Power Code One

With the Power of Self Love, All things are Possible

Question: In your life, is there anything that is not possible? Be honest. Are there any desires you have that you have had to relinquish because you think that they are not that important, it's too late to fulfill them, or you just can't fulfill them because of your current situation in life?

Take a few moments and make a list of these impossible to meet desires in your life.

_____

_____

_____

_____

_____

Now, let me ask you this. Is it possible that the things you have listed as impossible at this time may be possible at a time somewhere in the near or far future if a phenomenon were to occur? Keep in mind that we are filled with possibilities (a posse of abilities). Even in the word impossible, there is the idea of "I'm possible." Furthermore, through our relationships with others we have been abundantly blessed with an unlimited posse of abilities (possibilities).

So how did we get to the point where we limit the use of our possibilities? Remember every word has a meaning and because of this fact every word is mandated by universal law to produce according to it's meaning. Ignorance of the law does not excuse you from the law. It does not matter if you are conscious of the word's meaning or not, you will attract the meaning of the words you use back to you. There is a word that I have personally found myself using, even though I would speak about my unlimited possibilities frequently. This word is very familiar to many of us, the word is "can't." This word automatically states that there is something that is not possible, there is a limitation, and it is a marker in the mind to do not even make a move toward it because it will never happen. Can't is the language of people who feel powerless. When applying "can't" to your own and other's desires, what do you think will be the chances of you tapping into the full potential, resources and possibilities of your relationship with yourself and others? Just the simple subtraction of the word "can't" from your sentences and adding a word that denotes the desire to understand something, or being open to possibilities, draws out the abilities of all those involved in your relationship at that time. The first Power Code word for you to remember is **Reloving.** The word reloving means to recycle the love the universe has for you. Remember, we all really do love one another however we do not always know how to fully show it. So what we are recycling is the misunderstandings that develop from us not being fully aware of this innate love we all have for ourselves and one another.

I have often forgotten how much possibility exists, not just within myself, but also within my relationships with other human beings and the rest of the universe. We are all connected. We are all integral pieces of this gigantic puzzle called the universe. Without my piece or your piece, we would have to call the universe something else. In other words, it would not be the same.
There is a universal law that exists in ecology and it states that everything is to be used and nothing is to be wasted. Why is everything to be used? Everything is to be used because everything has a **purpose**; everyone and everything has a reason for being here. When we attempt to throw away or ignore any of our desires, feelings, interests, relationships and/ or experiences, we are not mentally working in harmony with the laws of the universe, and this makes learning our lessons harder than it has to be. We end up not enjoying what we attract, which equates to us not enjoying our life or our relationships. When we are blind to our use of the word can't, living a hard

life turns into a repetitive cycle. The more of our relationships we reject, the less we learn about ourselves. The less we learn about ourselves, the more we misunderstand ourselves, and because of this misunderstanding we are less motivated to embrace our whole selves. When we are in this state of mind we are also in doubt of our capabilities and usually conclude that we can not always get what we want. Even though we may conclude this, innately we know this is not true. **Here lies the root of all our internal conflict**. If we have concluded that we can not get what we want then we find ourselves constantly settling. We even pretend that we want what we are settling for because we have convinced ourselves that this is the best we can do therefore it is the best thing for us. This lesson is so important because in order to recycle our misunderstood lessons we must understand where they are originating from. Thus as long as this internal wrestling match continues all we will most commonly produce is more confusion. The more confusion we have in our lives the more we doubt ourselves. The key to recycling the chaos is to relove. Take a totally different approach to the experiences/relationships that you have deemed as no good for you. They are not preventing you from getting what you want. Look at them as the best thing that you could have ever asked for. Believe that they are the key to your strength, power, and mastery of you. Imagine this and you end the internal conflict. Can you now see how you have created all these lessons for yourself? When you truly understand that experiences are created from within and not from without then you have cracked the first power code and are on your way to fully expressing the most powerful language on the planet. The language is called Love 360 and is the language of self love. When you begin to direct your attention to the idea that you do have unlimited possibilities of getting what you truly desire, then you begin to instantly experience the rewards of Loving 360.

When we suppress any of our abilities, we are not demonstrating 100% self love. Instead, we are telling ourselves that there is a part of us that we do not want. Because of the precision and intricacies that make up our systems as human beings, every ability we possess is necessary to the identification of who we are as individuals. So if you were to get rid of an ability, then your whole system begins to compensate by signaling to you that your integrity is breached and there is a malfunction taking place. Your self signals to you in various ways; the most common one is through our emotions. The emotions that we have labeled as negative such as anger, depression, anxiety, frustration, apathy etc. are a few examples of the malfunctioning signals. Another example would be some form of physical pain or dis-ease, such as an ingrown toenail, common cold, headache, hypertension, diabetes or fibroids. Knowing this, it is important to realize that during these times we are only suppressing or misusing our abilities, we do not actually throw them away or lose them. The thing that has kept us trapped is our habit of ignoring our signals, instead of embracing and learning more about what message our selves are sending to us. Once ignoring ourselves becomes a way of life for us, we are at a point where we do not recognize our selves any more. And then we have to remember how to see, recognize and pay attention to our selves again.

Question: Is it true that what you put out is what you get back? If you put out disrespect (ignoring yourself) of your own power or possibilities, what will you get back?

What You Put Out is What you Get Back

Let us further examine this saying in more detail. What you put out is what you get back is referring to magnetic attraction and what we call back to ourselves in order to remember, learn and grow. Imagine the Universe as your personal university and your course of study is your life. The more you learn about your life, the more you grow in the knowledge of who you are. i.e. fulfill yourself. Your life is always seeking to fulfill itself. Therefore, if there is something you do not demonstrate understanding in, when you are given a personalized life test (a situation, a condition, experience etc.), the universe will give you homework based on that misunderstanding as well as an opportunity to take a re-test. We are all given homework until we make a 100% on our life's test. Then and only then do we move on to our next level in life. No one is allowed to flunk out. We are all connected, which means our growth affects one another. Life will give us as many opportunities to learn and grow as necessary. When we begin to resist the lesson, we start to create stress for ourselves; we become behind in our lessons, backed up on our assignments and it becomes overwhelming at times because it seems like it is to much for one person to complete. This is when we hear ourselves say it is hard to be ourselves and/or we do not have enough time to do personal work in order to achieve personal growth.

Life is very persistent with itself, remember you are life. No matter how much you may disrespect your life, you will always be given more opportunities to demonstrate your possibilities. Your life reloves you so why not relove your life?

Reloving is recycling the unconditional love that your life has for you.

Remember, Life's University grading system is unlike the grading system we currently have in place in our existing American school system. We are allowed to pass on to the next grade level without having mastered the current grade level we are in. We are given a passing grade with demonstrating a minimum understanding of at least 60 - 70% of the lesson. What about the other 30 - 40% of the information that we do not understand? By going on to the next level without this understanding, is it harder or easier for us to comprehend the next grade level of lessons?

Remember With the Power of Self Love All Things Are
Possible

Possibilities: an unlimited amount of abilities and/ or resources existing within life designed to create opportunities for us to get all of our desires met in any way imaginable.

"90% of what you do behind the scenes of your life is what prepares you to see and capitalize on your possibilities. So if you're waiting for applause from the outside world, you maybe waiting a very long time. You must learn to be your own cheerleader, for only you know the true progress you are making."

Always ReLove Yourself

Power Code Two

Powerful People are Patient

I am a New Orleans native and like most natives, I am a big Saints fan. Watching the Saints has taught me a lot, especially in the area of patience. Even though this may not be their intention, the Saints seem to play the game to have fun; they play as if they understand that sports are for recreation, fun and entertainment. However most fans call them the heart attack Saints because they have you on the edge of your seat until the last seconds of the game. I recall a particular game on September 26, 2004, with less than two minutes on the play clock; the Saints kicker had a chance to score three points that would put his team in a better position to secure the winning of the game. But what happened? He missed it, and sure enough, St. Louis scored a touchdown and tied the game, sending it into overtime at exactly 3:30 p.m. In overtime, the Saints had another opportunity to win the game, and guess what? They did! Even though it may look like you are losing sometimes, remember life is not over yet; you will always be given another opportunity to demonstrate your abilities to score. Remember 3:30 p.m. At this time everyday take an inventory of what you have been focusing on for that day, if your focus was on something other than what you wanted to achieve for the day refocus. You have not lost the opportunity to fulfill yourself. Stretch your patience with yourself and your "posse of abilities." Patience is something that we are all constantly developing as we grow and expand into doing bigger things. Patience allows us time to get know, mature and learn how to use our natural abilities.

In this lesson, we will focus on concentration, as it is essential to the growth and development of patience. Time, energy, focus and attention - all are words representing the tools needed for building mental concentration muscles.

Questions:
- Do you know what your main focus, goal or which ability you are learning to use at this time right now in your life?
- How much time, energy, and attention do you put into this current goal on a daily basis?
- Are you more concentrated on your life or someone else's?
- How much attention do you give to yourself on a daily basis? Give yourself a grade from 0% to 100%.
- How much attention do you pay to your inner voice (your personal teacher) that speaks to you all the time? Give yourself a grade from 0% to 100%.
- How often are you selfish? All the time, sometimes, every now and then, only on your birthday, never.

Over the annals of time selfishness has been given a very bad reputation. My goal for some time has been to become one of the most selfish people in our world. After you help me pick this word apart you will understand why selfishness is a monumental goal to achieve.

When you look at the word, **selfishness**, what do you see?
Self – is – h_____ ness (write this down)
There is an h that is left over from the spelling when we break this word down. What is the h for? (We will discuss the <u>h</u> in lesson three) For now let us focus on
Self – is – ness.

In your life, your **self is necessary** (Self- is-ness). Time, energy, and attention consistently applied to self are necessary for you to discover more about what you came to express in the world. Only you know what is in your heart and what you are feeling or thinking? Therefore, only you can express it accurately. Every time you fully express what's in your heart you get the opportunity to see who you really are.

So what does concentration and patience have to do with the Power Codes?

Concentration is important to our minds health. We use concentration to demonstrate our ability to be patient long enough to complete a lesson. When we complete a lesson, we can see the true value of our own strength and power. The real proof of mental strength is the measurement of how much more you understand yourself and your abilities. The bigger the ability, the more patience we have to develop to see our big ability make things happen.

In order to truly demonstrate patience you must have already mastered the ability to accept the things you can not change. One thing you surely can not change is the essence of who you are. When you are not conscious of who you are then it is easy for you to demonstrate a shortness of patience. When you are short on patience then it is vital to your overall well–being to get in the habit of repeating to yourself, "I accept the things I can not change." Once your mind is re-directed to this state of mind then you can begin to concentrate on learning more about the things you can change and gain a greater knowledge of your self (become more enlightened).

> "The important thing is to keep the important thing the important thing".
>
> Albert Einstein
>
> "Until you make peace with who you are, you will never be content with what you have"
>
> Doris Mortman

Challenge exercise: What big ability of yours are you not being patient with in your life right now? As soon as you understand that your patience is for you first and no one else, you will begin to see yourself manifest what you want in your life faster, easier and on a consistent basis.

A seven-day concentration diet that is very effective at developing patience and focus is <ins>The Listening Diet</ins>: Talk only when you are talking about yourself and truly listen to yourself. Read only if you are reading about yourself or seeking more information on a particular question you have asked yourself, as it relates to what you truly desire at this time. Listen for yourself when others are speaking-- this means seek to understand how what you are hearing applies to you. Do this for seven days. Practice, if necessary until you get it. Once you get it, then concentrate on doing this exercise for seven days, 24 hours a day. To maximize your learning process, keep a journal of the things you hear yourself say about yourself and what others say about you. *Sounds selfish doesn't it? Great! Remember it is ok to use the word "I" it truly is not a bad word like society makes it out to be. Without "I" there is no we. In reality "I" and "we" need each other.* For more information about the 7 Day Listening Diet Log on to www.soluniversity. com.

Keep in Mind: Your conditions and situations in life are your gyms where you work out your abilities, allow them to mature by learning how to maximally utilize them for their intended purpose.

Patience is concentrating on your abilities long enough to give them time to mature and facilitate you in getting precisely what your heart desires.

When you are being patient you are practicing **preloving**, that is, before you even see what your attraction has brought to you, you **love** it unconditionally. Prelove is a power code word, include it in your daily actions to become more familiar with the language and habits of the most Powerful People on the Planet. When in doubt prelove.

"In life our most powerful tool we have to create with is our imagination and those images that we act upon determines our Reality. So why not imagine that you are living the most beautiful life all the time and act upon that image."

Always Prelove Yourself

Power Code Three

Powerful People are Honest

After practicing the listening diet in power code two's lesson, hopefully you now know what the H stands for in Selfish. Self -is-H.
What do you think the H in Selfish stands?

Sometimes I think I know better, but when I am called upon to act out what I say I know, it turns out different from what I say I know. What am I overlooking here? What I have come to discover is that my self truly knows a lot of things innately, but because each moment is different, it is important to become fully present to each moment consistently so that you will know exactly how to fully apply yourself in that moment in order to produce the results you truly desire to experience consistently. There is no pre-programmed manual for the present; we create based upon a need to know basis in every moment. We are very effective in the present when we allow our whole selves to be fully present. This means keeping our attention on what we are feeling in the present, staying tuned in to it and expressing it. Staying tuned into your raw feelings vs. your emotions is a distinction you will come to master in power code three.

We create our own behavioral patterns. We have ones that lead to fulfillment and we have ones that lead to dissatisfaction. We are the only ones who know which behavior produces what. When we feel low in our own esteem and self trust, this a major clue that our behavior needs to evolve.

To further understand what it means to be fully present and tuned into your raw feelings; let us discuss the H in Selfish - it is a major indicator that lets you know when you are fully participating in the present. If you look at the word selfish closely, you will discover the H to mean <u>Self</u> – <u>is</u> – <u>H</u>onest. A truly selfish person is honest about what he or she is feeling and thinking all the time. Being honest about what you are feeling and thinking demonstrates honoring your feelings. My mother frequently says, "Feelings are real." Feelings are neither right nor wrong. They are a reality we are unable to escape. Furthermore, feelings represent someone's life. One thing is for sure, they are real to the person that possesses them. So when we are honest, we are sincerely expressing what we are feeling and thinking at any given moment. Because we do not always understand our feelings, our minds naturally ask ourselves questions: What does this feeling mean? And depending upon our relationship with our feelings we either further explore them, or we do not think about them and instead ignore them by misrepresenting them. Those feelings that we have determined unworthy of our love are those feelings that we have misrepresented by ascribing a negative or devaluing meaning to. It is these feelings that we are dishonoring and disrespecting. This method has proven to be very ineffective for us because by suppressing, hiding or denying our feelings, we do not move any closer to gaining a greater understanding of them. Also, because our feelings represent us, when we do not move toward understanding our feelings we do not progress toward gaining a greater understanding of ourselves.

Therefore, the most effective method of gaining a greater understanding of ourselves is to be open about what our feelings are communicating to us. When we do not understand them, we should ask more questions about what they mean, instead of trying to suppress or hide them. A more effective habit to develop is to fall in love with them (inlove them). Inlove is another power code word that is practiced by self love masters. **Inlove** means to acknowledge your feelings and become one with them. When you are inlove you are on "cloud nine." This is the best mental state to experience. In all actually when we are in this state of mind we have risen above emotions and are experiencing oneness with God.

Many of us assume that, because of our busy lifestyles, it takes too long to deal with our feelings, especially when our feelings are in an immature state. We often wonder when we will have the time to get to know our raw feelings when we often have a difficult time clearly expressing them to others. And to boot, people often seem as though they do not want to genuinely hear what we have to express. I do understand this very frequent dilemma however I must ask you this question, what is more valuable to you than what you are feeling? Since your feelings represent you, what else is more important in your life besides you? And do you think it is wise for you to hold back your feelings because of others?

Feelings are internal communications from our innate intelligence (also known as our spirit). We often confuse our feelings with our emotions. Emotions are our reactions to what we are feeling or thinking. We often say our feelings hurt. However it is not our feelings that are hurting rather what we experiencing is us trying to suppress, disguise or ignore what we are feeling. Powerless minded people often find themselves blaming others for hurting their feelings. Answer this question, when does is it make sense to ignore or suppress your innate intelligence?

When we are selfish, we truly understand the importance of being honest and inlove with our feelings. When we are not being honest about our feelings, we send out mixed signals to others. When we misrepresent our feelings, we disrespect them, and remember, what we put out is what we get back. If we put out disrespect for our feelings, guess what comes back to us? Disrespect 360.

Again we do not always understand our feelings or how to express them clearly at times. However, this is different from outright dishonesty. When we don't understand our feelings, then making them a topic of discussion for further examination is a great place to start. Taking responsibility for our own thoughts and feelings is a true sign of maturity.

Maturity is the appreciation of one's self, which overtime leads us to a greater understanding of ourselves and our abilities. When we constantly ignore or blame someone else for our feelings or emotions, our levels of understanding ourselves stay immature. As discussed above, a common practice that demonstrates a misunderstanding of our feelings is holding on to the idea that someone hurt our feelings, and, vice versa, that we hurt someone else's feelings. When we are not inlove with our feelings and do not view our own feelings as beautiful and worthy of fully expressing; this is a clear indication that we do not understand the difference between feelings and emotions yet. This misunderstanding is a power code lesson in your life that you need to focus on in order to grow beyond your present level of trust in your life.

Time to do some homework!

Have you ever heard yourself say, he or she hurt your feelings?

_____

If so, what did you mean? How did they hurt you? Give details.

_____
_____
_____
_____

Since your feelings are your personal guide (your innate intelligence), what do you think those feelings that you described above were instructing you to do?

_____
_____
_____
_____

Think about this: When do you notice your feelings the most? Your feelings are always being described in relationship to something else. The operative phrase is "in relationship." Your feelings are showing you which one of your many abilities is the most appropriate to apply in the present moment in every relationship. They are your inner messages telling you what to express, it is your inside telling your outside what to do. When you stay open to your feelings, you are actually staying open to your best ability to be applied to that moment. This is the reason you are in that particular relationship in the first place, to apply your abilities in a purposeful way. When you apply your natural abilities in a purposeful way, you feel useful, fulfilled and inlove.

Challenge: Identify a recurring unwanted "emotion" you have or are currently experiencing. It maybe one of rejection, pain, embarrassment, annoyance, disgust, anger, hurt, waste of time and/or sadness. Challenge yourself to start looking at this emotion as something necessary, valuable, and beautiful. Ask yourself, what is the reason for this emotion? What raw feeling is this emotion connected to? Why are you reacting to this raw feeling with this emotion? What can you learn from this emotion and feeling? (Remember, "feelings are real." They represent your most natural abilities.)

_____

_____

_____

_____

_____

_____

_____

A Case Study:
A social worker in the school system for 20 years keeps getting recurring feelings that it is time to retire and move on to do something else. Everyday, just the thought of going to work drains her energy. Her enthusiasm on the job is zero; even counseling the children feels like poking herself with needles. However, she consistently ignores her feelings because she thinks they are wrong. Besides, she only has five more years

to full retirement, and she assumes she should not have these thoughts about the children.

What do you think is really stressing her out?

_____

_____

_____

What do you think her distractions are?

_____

_____

_____

_____

Now, let us examine this common scenario together. Because she has ignored her feelings, there is some confusion about what her true feelings are. She thinks she has ill feelings towards her job and the children.

We know she has pigeon-holed her feelings because she is experiencing a roller coaster of emotions. Is it possible that her feelings are actually telling her how to reach fulfillment. Let us help Ms. Social Worker view the messages she's sending herself in a completely different way. Ms. Social Worker, please consider this: could your feelings be expressing to you that it is time to move on from this position, but because you do not understand your feelings and the role they play in your life, you are reacting to them with doubt and fear, and taking it out on the job and the children. Instead of asking, "what does this mean" or saying "let me go and explore what my intelligence is guiding me to," you are taking the disobedient route. You keep ending up where all disobedient people go – self-punishment or hell on earth. Self-punishment is the equivalent of being stressed out, in doubt and unfulfilled on a consistent basis. It definitely looks completely different from being inlove with self. The longer you disobey, the longer your punishment time.

Does this story sound familiar to you?

_____

So what would you suggest to Ms. Social Worker to get her out of her self-punishment, or hell on earth? Remember to *be fair* with Ms. Social Worker as you give her steps to get out of and stay out of self-punishment.

_____

_____

_____

Honesty = honoring your feelings and being fully open about your understanding of them. Honesty is designed to emphasize the particular lesson you are engaged in at any given time.

"The truth is we never really fall in love with other people, we fall in love with the feeling that we have when we are around them or think about them."

Inlove Yourself Always

Transition

Are you experiencing a flood of emotions are or you clear about your feelings right now? Whatever you are experiencing right now fully embrace it.

Does it feel like you are in transition? Or in Limbo?

Great! This means you are actively shifting right now. You are shifting your attention. No more hiding what you assume makes you look bad to others. They really do not care at any rate. They have their own issues to contend with and your life is just entertainment to them, just like theirs is to you. You are now aware of the necessity of focusing more of your attention on yourself. Crossing over to the consistent fulfillment side of life maybe a little rough at first, depending on what particular emotions and insecurities you are dealing with. However, let me reassure you that the journey is so worth it. Once you fully "cross over," by completing the ultimate shift in your attention, you will ask yourself what took you so long and why in the world would anyone choose to not live in Heaven on earth all the time.

"The Concept of sickness extends beyond illnesses that afflict the body. It includes the "poor health" of a business, an "ailment" in a relationship, and emotional "illnesses" such as anxiety and depression. With the right tool, we can heal all manner of dis-ease."

Yehuda Berg, The 72 Names of God

Cracking the Power Codes releases the energy needed for healing at the deepest and most profound level of your being. Incorporating the Power Codes in your daily activity represents you are taking full responsibility for your life, enjoying it and inspiring others to fully activate their power and love themselves fully too! Welcome to the world of the Most Powerful People on the Planet. Welcome to Heaven on Earth. Congratulations. Everyone is called however only a few choose to enter Heaven with both feet.

Thank you.

Power Code Four

Powerful People are Fair

Masters of self love treat all parts of themselves equally. When parts of our self are treated equally with 100% acceptance, a harmonious balance exists that resonates throughout our entire being. We feel unconditionally loved, meaning we experience full and complete acceptance of ourselves no matter what the conditions.

As previously mentioned, there is a grand universal law that exists which states, "All is to be used, nothing and no one is to be wasted. " This universal law sets the tone for treating all things equally. Since all energy is to be used and nothing is to be wasted, this must mean that everything has a purpose. What purpose have you given your feelings? Is that purpose in line with the universal law? Is the purpose you have given to your feelings in line with the natural design of feelings? Is the purpose you have given to your feelings causing you to treat all of your feelings equally, or is it causing you to waste a great majority of your feelings?

The following questions you are about to be asked may stop you in your tracks. This is what they are designed to do.

If you are ignoring, disobeying, or wasting a great majority of your feelings, and your feelings represent your unique innate intelligence, then *whose intelligence are you using to guide your daily actions?*

Since we are always thinking about something, then *whose intelligence are you thinking about?*

Another way of asking yourself this question is, *whose feelings are you most frequently getting to know better?*

_____

_____

If you are consistently thinking about someone else's feelings, does that bring you closer to learning more about you or the other person? _____

How does learning more about others feelings get you closer to what you want in life and accomplishing the goals that you have set for yourself?

_____

If a person does not consistently apply his or her own intelligence in any given situation, would you say they are of sound mind or of an unstable mind?

_____

Are you of sound mind? _____ yes _____ no
What does having a sound mind mean to you?

_____

_____

_____

Describe what having an unstable mind means to you.

_____

_____

_____

_____

_____

I can remember the first time someone asked me if I was of sound mind. I was about 23-years-old. I was at an attorney's office hoping he would help me get out of a jam. How did I end up at his office? I was in the process of purchasing a new car because the one I had at the time was an unsightly wreck, damaged by a fleeting car, but drivable and fully paid for. At the time I only had liability insurance. Since I was considering getting it fixed, which I would have to pay for it myself, my father suggested I look for another car. His idea sounded wonderful to me. I was a full-time podiatric medical student, without a job, and living on student loans. Even though I had no idea what car I wanted to buy or how I was going to pay for it, I still decided to go and shop around. The first dealership I went to I ended up in the car they wanted me to have, with a monthly car payment that was outrageously outside of my means. What happened? The very cute and charming salesman told me to take the fancy car home for the weekend and see if I really liked it. So I signed papers and off I went. After joy-riding over the weekend, reality set in, and the following Monday, I returned the car. The very cute and charming salesman greeted me and I explained to him my decision. He said: "I am sorry, my dear, you signed the papers and the car is yours to keep, besides, we have already sent your old car to our other car lot for re-sale. " In shock, I asked to speak to his manager and the car dealership owner. They both told me the same thing. I was stuck. After telling my story to several family members and friends who agreed with me that I had been scammed, my cousin referred me to her attorney for help. I arrived at the attorney's office, explained to him my story and showed him the papers. He asked me one question: Were you of sound mind when you signed these papers? Of course I said yes because I knew I was not crazy (so I thought at the time). And his final statement was, "Then there is nothing I can do for you."

> I thought I was of sound mind at the time but was I really?

I am so grateful for the above experience, as much as I wanted to cry and blame others for my uncomfortable experience; I knew it was time for me to grow up. I realized I was being called upon to become more mature not only physically but mentally and spiritually as well.

The English language dictionary's meaning for the word sound is "stable, a vibration." Does your mind hear an inner sound? Do you hear a unique voice of your own? When you hear this unique voice is it stable? Do you feel a harmonious vibration resonate through out your entire being when your unique voice speaks, similar to when you are listening to your favorite song?

Saying we are of sound mind means we are aware of our feelings, our own natural intelligence, our unique voice and our true desires. When we ignore our desires, we do not hear what our feelings are communicating to us about ourselves, causing our thinking to be out of alignment with ourselves. When our thinking is not in alignment with our natural intelligence, we are only able to exhibit reactionary behavior, which is very unstable. This is how we can find ourselves in a situation and wonder how in the world we got there, leaving us to think that we are not the responsible party. I know from experience that it is very difficult to take responsibility for putting yourself in a condition that appears not to be in your favor. The funny part is the only way to get out of the unwanted condition is to take full responsibility for the condition.

In my example above, I was not a victim. The main issue or distraction was that I did not know what I wanted. I was not of sound mind at the time, meaning I was not allowing my own innate intelligence guide me. I was not fully inlove with my own intelligence. Therefore, I was following someone else's intelligence leading me to the conclusion that I was scammed. But in reality I was right where I needed to be, in a jam so that I could learn the value of my own intelligence and the role it plays in my fulfillment. I had to learn how to be full of my own intelligence, fulloving. **Fulloving** is another power code word to practice; it is the act of unconditionally taking total ownership for every part of our lives. Of course, it took some time for me to actualize this lesson. However, as you can tell, it was a memorable lesson for me, one of those turning point lessons – a major breakthrough in the understanding of the habits of powerful people. I learned to be fair with all of my life lessons by treating them all equally. Treating them all equally means taking full responsibility for all of my life lessons for it is the key to consistently evolving in integrity and maturity.

"When we are able to embrace every condition of our lives with equal enthusiasm then we can say we truly know what it means to feel powerful and fully loved."

Fullove Yourself Always

Power Code Five

Powerful People are Responsible

A sound mind as discussed in power code lesson four is a mind that obeys its spirit, its innate intelligence. When you express what your spirit conveys to you, you are being responsible. You are taking full responsibility for the fulfillment of your unique purpose and reason for being present here on Earth. You have one job to do here on earth while you live, and that one job is to express your original, unique, one-of-a-kind intelligent self. This is the agreement you made with yourself and all other beings before you manifested your physical appearance here on earth. When you fully embrace the unique individual role you play in respect to all others, you truly understand that it is natural to be different. Being different becomes the standard way of living and pretending to be the same as others just so you can fit in becomes the outcast way of being.

Many of us consider ourselves to be very responsible people; we take care of duties at work, at home, we make sure our parents and children are well, and we pay our bills. However, at the end of the day, what have we truly accomplished? How much of an impact have we made on the collective growth and maturity of our lives and in the world? What have we realized about ourselves and our purpose on a daily basis? If you were to take an inventory of your unique purpose fulfillment to-do list, how many check marks would you have on your list on a daily basis?

Basic Unique Purpose To–do List:
- ✓ Love my Spirit
- ✓ Love my Mind
- ✓ Love my Body
- ✓ Love Others (Relationships)

Keeping it simple is an effective strategy that has worked for centuries. In order to keep it simple, we have to be aware of the basic nutrients required to nourish our whole selves. We know we have a spirit, mind, and body. In addition everyone is also in some type of relationship with others. When we are being responsible for ourselves we provide excellent nutrition and exercise for all aspects of ourselves, which keeps us in balance allowing us to experience consistent excellent health, wellbeing, and fulfillment.

Now here is a very important question: what is the best food for your spirit and how do you demonstrate love to your spirit? When you consciously feed your spirit the best nutrient, it sets the tone for the health and wellbeing of your mind, body and relationships. Yes you may read very inspiring books, listen to the most motivating speeches, exercise your body and eat as healthy as you can; however, how do you know when you have fully fed your spirit?

If you are not aware of the best food for your spirit, how effective can you be at carrying out your daily responsibilities?

In the spaces provided below:

1. List the best nutrient that fully feeds your Spirit:

_____

_____

2. Write down the ways you show love to your spirit.

_____

_____

_____

_____

Talk to your spirit and ask your spirit for the answer. Be Patient. Listen intently for the answer. I know as a responsible person you do not want another day to go by without fully feeding your spirit. Please respond to your spirit's call immediately, for not feeding your spirit properly has a deleterious effect on your mind, body, and all of your relationships.

In order for you to holistically mature, your spirit requires of you the same type of care you show when you are taking full responsibility for your role as a parent, which lets your child know you love them; or when you complete all your duties at work showing that you are mature enough to handle the job. When you are fully feeding your spirit you demonstrate the same type of full responsibility indicating that you truly love yourself. **Truloving** is another power code word and something that real responsible and mature people demonstrate regardless of their earthly age. Truloving is responsibly taking care of your spirit, mind, body and relationships' daily nutritional requirements. In reality no one can fully feed you but you.

This is why there is a New Golden Rule:

LOVE YOURSELF THE WAY YOU WANT OTHERS TO LOVE YOU

Now have you figured out what the most nutritious food for your spirit is yet? ___ yes ___ no

"I can give you diamonds and I can give you pearls, but if I have not fed my spirit lately I will not be able to truly love you."

Trulove Yourself Always

Power Code Six

Powerful People are Attentive

When your inner voice speaks to you, who hears it? Does the person sitting next to you hear it? Does your mother or father hear it? No one else hears your inner voice but you. Why do you think this is? Do others need to hear what your self is teaching you about you, or do they have their own inner voice teaching them about them? What happens all too often is that we sometimes think our inner voice is teaching us about other people, not realizing that our inner voice is designed to remind and teach us only about ourselves.

If you are constantly trying to figure out what other people are feeling, thinking, or need, when do you have time to pay attention to and express your full self? Just like school teachers, in order to be effective at getting their lesson across they need their students' attention. Our personal teacher, our spirit, requires our mind's attention. Our undivided attention is the only nutritious meal for our spirit.

When you do not pay attention to your spirit (your intelligence), you are distracted. Today, many people, children and adults, are diagnosed with ADD (Attention Deficit Disorder) and Affluenza. The diagnosis of ADD and Affluenza makes so much sense; however, there is a root cause to these diagnoses that is not frequently addressed. It is often said that many people may have ADD and not know it. If you are ignoring your spirit on a consistent basis, then yes there is an attention deficit present. Be that as it may, the question is who or what are you not giving your attention to? It is apparent that there is no real shortage of attention itself because we are always paying attention to something which becomes very apparent in the Wikipedia's definition of Affluenza .

> **affluenza,** n. a painful, contagious, socially transmitted condition of overload, debt, anxiety and waste resulting from the dogged pursuit of more.

affluenza, n. 1. The bloated, sluggish and unfulfilled feeling that results from efforts to keep up with the Joneses. 2. An epidemic of stress, overwork, waste and indebtedness caused by the pursuit of the American Dream. 3. An unsustainable addiction to economic growth.

As I mentioned earlier if you are not paying attention to your spirit then it is your spirit that is short on attention. So, yes many people are suffering from ADD but the complete name of the disorder is what I like to call **SADD** (Self Attention Deficit Disorder). SADD develops full blown overtime when your own natural intelligence is not the highlight of your life. Because we all operate from some form of intelligence, if you are not using your own then you must be using an artificial intelligence. When you are using an artificial intelligence to direct your life this is known as distraction. When in distraction mode you are on the path of being SADD. And when one is being SADD they are unaware of their unique purpose and desires. The main thing about SADD that makes it so sad is that, one is not getting what they want simply because they are unable to recognize it, even when it is staring them right in the face. If you have SADD then it is critical that you recognize the fact that you are carrying and operating from an **Artificial Intelligence Virus (A.I.V.)**. A.I.V. prevents you from recognizing, listening to and hearing your internal unique voice. Your unique voice represents your spirit/innate intelligence. If you think you are suffering from A.I.V. please contact our office immediately and also continue to read this book.

Contact information:
Stephanie@relationshipfitnesscenter.com or soluniversity@ therealhelp.com

Is your Spirit Starving for your attention?

I am sure by now you know the answer to the previous question in lesson number five. The basic food nutrient your spirit requires is your attention. When we ignore our spirit, it signifies that we do not understand the awesome power we contain within ourselves. Thus causing us to think thoughts of less than or greater than instead of equal to whatever we see on the outside of us. When we are not truloving and fully feeding our spirit, consequently, we attract lessons to ourselves to assist us with paying more attention to ourselves so that we can see more of our magnificence.

To recap from power code one, the huge difference between the school of life and the traditional American school system is that in life, we do not go on to our next lesson until we thoroughly understand our current one. Traditional school systems allow us to continue on to our next lesson even though we may not fully comprehend our current lesson. We can score a 70% grade and still go on to our next lesson. What about the 30% we did not understand? How will that affect our understanding at the next level? This system may work to produce minimum satisfactory results; however, in the universe's school of life, due to the delicate balance of our inter connectedness with one another and our innate drive to transform and evolve, understanding 100% of our current life lesson is the minimum requirement for moving on to our next grade level in the University of Life.

Why does our spirit feed off of our attention?
Our spirit has a specific role to play in our lives and it is to guide us. Our spirit navigates us through our lives and helps us make the best decisions for ourselves as we are remembering and learning about ourselves through our life experiences. The more attention we pay to our spirit the more knowledge and wisdom it shares with us. If we are not paying attention to our spirit then this means we are not showing an interest in learning more about our real selves, therefore, our unique spiritual information is not needed at that time. Think about that. This is important for you to understand right now, especially if you have contracted A.I.V and are SADD.

Now that you have identified the role of your spirit which is to serve as your personal guide, there must be a part of yourself that your spirit is guiding and plays the role of a student. This student has the responsibility of listening, obeying and learning from its personal teacher, its spirit. I am sure you already know the answer. Yes, it is your mind.

How effective can you be at learning, if your mind is frequently distracted?
In order to effectively learn more about yourself, you must pay full attention to yourself. Many of us are in the habit of listening to our spirit the way we pretend to listen to others. Just because we are not talking when they are talking does not mean we are genuinely listening, with all ears. Did you know that we have inner ears and outer ears?

> A key component to paying attention is listening.

We usually pay attention in order to learn something. When we are actively involved in learning, we listen for the sake of gaining a greater understanding of ourselves. When we are paying attention to ourselves, our mind processes information from what we hear internally from our spirit as well as what we hear externally with our physical ears. This is called listening with allears. When we are **Allearsloving,** we are undividedly paying attention to the wisdom from within as well as what our wisdom is attracting and reflecting back to us from without. Allearsloving is the sixth power code word that awakens the Love 360 language that is naturally present within all of us.

Now that you have identified the basic nutrient for the spirit:

1. What is the basic food nutrient for the mind?

    _____

    _____

2. How do you demonstrate love to your mind?

    _____

    _____

    _____

    _____

    _____

"When we are in the habit of loving learning and listening with all ears, it is much easier to accept all and enjoy life to its fullest."

Allearslove Yourself Always

Power Code Seven

Powerful People are Open to Learning (Accepting)

Do you love learning? Why or why not?

_____

_____

_____

What do you love learning about?

_____

_____

_____

Do you love Homework? Why or why not?

_____

_____

_____

How often do you do homework and what type of homework do you do?

_____

_____

_____

Sometimes our relationship with learning is not so welcoming because of the way we have been accustomed to viewing our lessons. When we have a difficult lesson, learning can sometimes be viewed as a punishment. We also have been socialized into labeling our life lessons as good or bad. And when we are inside of a "bad" or "tough" lesson then we assume that we have done something wrong and are embarrassed about exposing our lessons to others because they may think we are a bad person. It is definitely time to evolve our collective meaning of a lesson and its relationship to learning.

Traditional grammar, high school, and/or college has its role to play in our lives as human beings. It was originally designed to prepare us for a job in society not to educate us on being great human beings. There are many jobs we can acquire today and they are many schools we can choose to attend in order to develop the necessary skills to be efficient and good at doing our jobs. For the most part all it takes is being able to memorize information and demonstrate that we have been taught the information by being able to regurgitate a minimum of 70% of the information on a standardized test. It is not important whether or not you truly learned the information and are able to practically apply it to your natural purpose in life. So why am I bring up this point? It is important for all of us to understand and make the distinction between learning and being taught to memorize. Learning takes place through the process of education, which means to draw from within. Being taught to memorize facts about what other human beings intelligence has conveyed to them is an out to in process. Without proper guidance (allearsloving) this type of process can breed AIV and SADD. And it will set up an internal war within self. And this inner war will be the source of the person's distractions in life.

Yes one may graduate from a prestigious school and acquire a high paying job in society however that does not exempt them from having SAD Disorder (no inner peace). What will exempt them and guard them from SADD is developing and maintaining peace within. Of which many of us know as HAPPY. True happiness occurs within and is radiated without. When there is no war going on within the essence of who we are shines through clearly and is felt by ourselves and others. These are the people we recognize as having attained a state of serenity, peace, personal power, prosperity, nirvana and/or heaven on earth.

Currently the United States is in a nationwide school crisis. What people will come to realize is that the original design for the public school system in existence today is out-dated and has exhausted its need. The human beings of present day society are in need of more than job skills. The majority of human beings of today are massively suffering from A.I.V. and SADD. And developing only job skills will not alleviate the pain and suffering associated with the SAD Disorder, it only exacerbates it.

> Could a negative attitude toward learning and failing schools have anything to do with the subject matter one is studying?

As Grace Lee Boggs stated in one of her 2011 television interviews, the nation is in need of some deep changes. These deep changes will have to come from within the depths of individuals which is where true power lies. People will have to re-think there relationships, meaning we as human beings will have to become more accountable to how we treat ourselves and others. Every issue we are having in the world at its root is a relationship issue. So it stands to reason that if we are to make any real progress as a nation we are going to have to seek Real Help and focus our attention on becoming more Relationship Fit. This fitness will only happen through formal Relationship and Life Skills Education. Just as technology gets outdated, so does our thinking and what we understand at any given time. So, to stay effective and current with the evolving changes in the world, we have to be open to them. No matter what our age or mental health status, we all have the capacity to recall and learn. *Learning is the basic food nutrient for our mind.* We get mentally charged up when we learn something that is very useful to us. It is at these times we feel a sense of our own power, i.e. fulfilled, at peace and in harmony.

So, what is learning?

_____

_____

_____

We know we are all on this earth for a particular reason. No one is here to do nothing. We all have a purpose. **Learning** is all about becoming aware of your unique purpose and gaining a greater understanding how you function at your very best. And through this understanding we wisely do our purpose more effectively every day. When we adhere to what our great teacher is teaching us, we stay fully abreast of our individual missions. In my experience, the most difficult part of learning in this manner is that we sometimes get confused about distinguishing between and interpreting the messages of our spirit and the messages of others we see and hear externally. What is the purpose of those external messages we have attracted to ourselves and how do we best apply them to our lives? In other words, how do we pay attention to what's going on inside as well as what is going on outside of us? How do we master the powerful people habit of allearsloving?

Let us look at it like this: View your spirit as the C.I.A. (Central Intelligence Agency) and your mind as the elected president of your purpose, this analogy may help to simplify the distinction.

The first thing you must know and accept is the fact that you were unanimously selected by all of the beings in the universe to do a unique job in the universe. You were selected because of the unique way you think; it is perfect for the one-of-a-kind job you were chosen for and have been unanimously elected to do. And based on that job you are also given your own intelligence (C.I.A.) that assists you personally with fulfilling your job.

Once you understand this first fact, it allows your mind to accept and appreciate itself for who it is and the way it thinks at all times.

The second fact you must understand is that you are not aware of everything, nor are you expected to be aware of everything, which is why you possess the innate ability to learn. Because we live in a shifting world and things are constantly changing and evolving, it would be very distracting to be aware of everything that is going on at one time in the world. Therefore, this is why you are supplied with information on a need-to-know basis, based on the lesson you are learning or the job you are doing at that time.

Once you are comfortable with the fact that you do not need to know everything, and that there are a lot of things you will not be aware of at any given time, you are able to focus and concentrate a whole lot easier on the task at hand.

Thirdly, as you get a grip on the second fact, that you do not need to be aware of everything, you will be able to wisely utilize whatever you attract to yourself at any given moment. This act alone will facilitate your learning process a whole lot faster. You will also no longer second guess or stress yourself out trying to figure out if what you are attracting is good or bad for you. Remember, the law of ecology, all is to be used nothing is to be wasted. Staying in tune with this law takes the guess work out of what to keep and what to throw away. *Staying focused on the job we have the desire to do and have been called to do is an automatic cure for indecision, procrastination and distraction.*

When you have reached a point where you are consistently in this president and C.I.A. type of learning zone you are in a trusting mind set. A trusting mind set **A**ccepts, openly loves and learns from everything. A trusting mind is an **openloving** mind. **Openloving** is trusting the fact that everything is working in your favor to assist you with your growth and fulfillment all the time. In order to be open to learning, our minds have to be strong at openloving. Think about it, how much will you learn if you are not open to your teacher. When you are not open and trusting, you are in doubt and insecure about the lessons being presented to you. And when you are in doubt or insecure about something, you protect yourself from it by defending yourself, and are thus unable to relax in its presence. It is a fact that when we are stressed mentally we stop learning and we automatically go into survival mode. Openloving is a power code habit that shifts one from survival mode to fully living mode.

In order to effectively learn and make learning fun, we have to Trust.

No Trust = No Learning

Trust and you can learn and have fun at the same time. The school and workplace environments will look totally different if every student and staff member understood this lesson wouldn't it?

How many people do you trust?

_____

Why do you trust them?

_____
_____
_____

Those whom you do not trust, why don't you trust them?

_____
_____
_____

When you are around those you do not trust describe your behavior and how you feel when you are around them.

_____
_____
_____

Do you think trust is a key component to building relationships? Why or why not?

_____
_____
_____

Accepting is being open to learning. Learning is becoming more aware of your purpose and gaining a greater understanding of how you function at your very best.

"Be open and trust the fact that everything in the universe was and is being created to assist you with fulfilling you."
OpenLove Yourself Always

Power Code Eight

Powerful People are Powerful

Trust in the universal laws that are in existence because they are in place so that everyone has equal opportunities to attain fulfillment. **Everything is created by God and therefore everything is perfect, great, and excellent. Everything in existence comes from God and therefore is God, even you.**

Before we go any further at looking into the relevance of this statement, it is first imperative for you to answer the following questions:

Do you believe the above bold statement? _____ yes _____ no

What does the above statement mean to you?

_____

_____

_____

List some things that are not included in the everything that God created and explain your answer.

_____

_____

_____

God loves all. No matter how you slice and dice it, I have researched what God means to people from all over the world and found one commonality. God is the most consistent name used to represent our universal spirit, the voice of our intelligence, the creator of life, and the source of all our power. God is irrespective of religions and/or spiritual beliefs.

> God= Life = Universal = All

God loves all so God consistently works for all to evolve and grow; there are no exceptions. With this concept in mind, GOD can be translated to mean the _Giver of Desires;_ this is the main way God shows love for all of us. Innately we all know that God wants all of us to grow and expand.

Let us look more in depth into the concept of God as the _Giver of Desires_ – because God gives us our desires, there is no reason to doubt any of our desires. When God gives us our desires, we can rest assured and trust that everything we need to support our desires is also provided.

When we naturally desire something, there is a common saying amongst believers that states, "Whatever you are truly desiring believe you already have it." All of our natural desires are connected to us fulfilling our purpose for being here. Understand that and you understand the root of your power and your strengths. _When we are in doubt about our desires, then the question to ask yourself is, is this what you want from your heart, or is this something someone told you need or should want for yourself and you are assuming that you desire it._

In order to fully understand and demonstrate power, you have to trust that all of your natural desires are worthy of fulfilling, and must be fulfilled, in order to grow and mature yourself. You are here to fulfill your desires. When you fulfill your desires you are happy. This is a simplified formula of how the universal system is designed to ensure and encourage all of us to continually evolve ourselves.

> Our relationship to our desires determines our level of maturity, quality of living and quantity of fulfillment.

Once we actualize the understanding that it is our desires (whether we are conscious of them or not) that run the whole system of the Laws of Attraction, then we will begin to look at everything we attract into our lives completely different. The amount of time and work we put into studying our desires determines what we put out, and what we put out is what we get back. This means whatever level we understand and embrace our desires is what we will express and according to our level of understanding and acceptance of our desires, it will determine the next lesson we attract to ourselves to assist us with further understanding our desires. For example, a small business owner is desiring to increase their clientele drastically through a mass marketing campaign. The small business owner has been in business for four years and has some knowledge about how to market to their clientele however they are not quite clear yet, otherwise they would have already done it. So as they proceed to study and market to their target consumer, they attract lessons back to them that can assist them with being more successful at marketing to their target and increase their bottom line, i.e. more clientele equates to more income. Now what do you think would happen to their level of understanding if they become distracted from their original desire, especially during "tough" lessons?

The next question is designed to ensure that you get this lesson:

When is it appropriate to reject what you have attracted into your life? Why?

_____

_____

_____

Because of our preconceived notions and societal standards we tend to quickly reject those things and circumstances that do not look like what we thought they were supposed to look like. Those things are usually considered ugly, negative and worthy of rejection. The first thing we must understand about attraction is, it is designed by and always adheres to universal law. It is fixed in its nature. It is not based on what we do not want; it is based solely on what we desire and are truly interested in at any given time. Our attractions are designed to draw out and build upon our strengths.

So what does this mean and what does it have to do with us feeling powerful?

When we understand and align our thinking with the universal nature of the law of attraction, then it becomes quite easy for us to be in tune with our unique purpose for being here on earth and fulfilling ourselves. We consistently feel our power when we are trusting everything that we attract into our lives. We feel our power during these times because by being open to our attractions we are able to fully see ourselves and our strengths. We do not have to understand all the minute details of how and why we attracting what we are attracting while we are in the moment that is what trusting is all about. As long as you are in constant pursuit of your desires the how and why naturally comes to you. This is called the process of Loving 360. Being in constant pursuit of your desires reflects a great love for yourself and when you are putting out this great love into the universe all you will attract back (360) to yourself is love.

Here is a little nugget of wisdom for you to remember when you are inside of a rejection lesson: when you think you are being rejected, you are really repelling what you are not interested in at that time and are being re-directed to focus your attention on your strengths and what you truly desire to experience.

Trusting that the universal laws are always working in our favor makes fulfilling ourselves a whole lot easier. This understanding brings on an evolved meaning of the motto "In God We Trust." When we really learn to trust everything then we are godloving. **Godloving is understanding and trusting that we always attract to us what we are truly desiring.** Godloving is a powerful habit practiced by powerful people. You may hear people say they love everyone however what you may not be aware of is the mindset of people who truly demonstrate a love for all people. Those who genuinely love all people have a godloving mindset. And with this type of mindset it is easy to love and trust everyone.

Now are you clear about the law of attraction? If you are not sure, it will definitely affect your loyalty to your Godself. The minute someone appears to reject, repel, or redirect you, notice how you respond and you will definitely know then how much you understand the law of attraction and how to godlove. Utilize the exercise on the next page to measure your understanding of the law of attraction.

"Without trust in everything there is no real expression of a true love for God and that definitely interferes with enjoying life to its fullest and having fun."
Godlove Yourself Always

Understanding the Law of Attraction

For the next 7 days, keep a log of your response to what you attract and measure your level of true power (fulfillment) you felt for that day on a scale of 0% -100%. True Power is being able to utilize your natural strengths in order to achieve a desired outcome.

My True Power Report Card

Day	The challenging experience I attracted today	My response to what I attracted	My True Power Grade
1			
2			
3			
4			
5			
6			
7			

Power Code Nine

Powerful People are Loyal

The greatest secret about attaining Peace, Power and Prosperity is discovered here in Power Code Lesson nine. What is the greatest secret? Say it out loud.

Be loyal to your desires and your desires will prove their loyalty to you.

This is a self love law. It is the key to living the peaceful, powerful and prosperous life you were born to experience.

Understanding this law surpasses the day to day routine way of attempting to live a full life. Fully applying this law is the true mark of the most powerful people on the planet. Applying the self love law means you are loyal to your desires. When you are loyal to your desires, your desires will prove their loyalty to you. Your desires are designed to strengthen, empower and fulfill you. Fully embracing your hearts desires is a marker of Self Love.

As you embrace more of your hearts desires on a daily basis, you will also evolve your understanding of who is determining the fulfillment of your purpose, mission, experiences and outcomes. You will also come to realize that the more of yourself you fully accept and apply, the more your actions, as well as what you produce, will always reflect a higher level of trust, appreciation, loyalty, and most of self-love. You will then earn and be promoted to the next milestone of life, which is being an inspiration to others. People listen more to those who genuinely love and accept themselves and others for who they are unconditionally. When we constantly blame others for our misfortunes, or attempt to change or control them, we automatically turn others off to us, demonstrating that we have lost sight of the reason why we have attracted them into our lives in the first place. This is a sure sign that we are not being loyal to our desires.

When we are loyal to our desires we gain clarity, insight, wisdom, understanding and a deeper sense of connection to ourselves and others.

Loyalty benefits ALL: being loyal has a farther-reaching impact than many of us realize. As you grow and truly understand something, those around you also grow in their understanding to that something because you are able to clearly share your understanding through your words, actions, and experiences. And in turn those who you have connected with spread what they have learned to others, who also spread it to others and so on. All of this evolution manifested because one powerful person was loyal to his or her desire. I am confident that the next powerfully inspiring person to assist with the evolution of us all will be YOU.

<u>ALL- One</u>
On the Tree of Life
We are one Big Family
Connected by one main Desire
To Express and Enjoy Life to its Fullest

Before we expect for others to be loyal to us and follow us, let us prove to ourselves that we have enough internal power to influence and inspire ourselves first. Leading yourself into the direction you truly desire to experience is the mark of true loyalty and inspiring leadership. When you see yourself doing less talking and more being in order to get a point across, then you know you have been promoted to being an inspired Leader.

What about being loyal to others?
If you are loyal to yourself, you are automatically loyal to others. This is what spreadloving is all about. **Spreadloving** is being

one with your desires and inspiring others to be one with theirs too. Spreadloving is a contagious action. Spreadloving is another power code word that opens the flood gates to a multitude of Love 360 language words and actions.

What Happens when I am not loyal to Myself?
When you are not loyal to your desires your time and energy is applied to something other than what it is naturally intended for. The pursuit of your hearts desires are mentally put on hold, and because it is our desires that provide us with strength and vitality for living, you will eventually manifest a sense of powerlessness, disconnection, mental and/or physical body stress, illness and disease.

Please note that in the above it is stated that our desires are put on hold *mentally*. Emphasis is put on the word mentally because in reality our desires are still present we just do not see them at that time. Remember the Law of Attraction: You are always attracting what you truly desire consciously or unconsciously.

What can you do to re-build strength in being loyal to yourself and restore your sense of power, connection and well being, mentally, physically and spiritually?
In order to re-build and restore your health you must first make an uncommon commitment to Love 360. We all want our hearts desires to be fulfilled. Staying focused on our desires is the challenge that the Love 360 language makes easy for you. Knowing precisely what you desire is connected to a Relationship Fitness Skill called Seeing Yourself First. This skill requires strength in adhering to the Self Love Law: Be Loyal to Your Desires.

How do I truly know when I am being loyal to my desires?
When you have completed something unique to you and have mastered it, your embodiment of this uniqueness is a marker letting you know that you are being loyal. Mastering your

uniqueness shows that you are paying attention to your whole self even your blind spots. It also says that you have courageously embraced those so called unsightly aspects of yourself long enough allowing those aspects to demonstrate to you there value and connection to your consistent fulfillment.

Some other indicators are being aware of your unique purpose, your strengths and fully utilizing them. Also when you have no doubt in yourself you know you are being loyal to your hearts desires.

A True Demonstration of Loyalty

A common scenario: Imagine that you have joined a group of people in the local community. The group has decided to work together on a specific project. The project idea represents the collective desires of all parties involved. Therefore, the conglomerate has collective responsibilities that must be taken care of in order for the project to evolve. Each person in the group has decided to take responsibility for a particular part of the project. About one month into the project you begin to have conflicting issues with some of the members in the group, wherefore, you begin to slack off on your interest in the project, even though this was something you said you desired and felt greatly inspired to do. You have discussed your concerns with the members of the group on several occasions. However, the members who you have conflict with continue to do what they have been doing which is the one thing that is frustrating you and now you are considering resigning from the group. Imagine that this is you in this scenario, what would be the first thing you would ask yourself? And why?

_____

_____

_____

What advice would you give yourself if you came to you and asked you how would you proceed?

_____

_____

_____

Here are the first questions that I would ask you:
Are you sure that this project is what you are truly desiring to experience? If so, then what happened to your loyalty to your desire? If this is not your real desire, then what are you truly desiring to experience?

Now that you are aware of the Power of Being Loyal to your desires how would you handle the conflict with your team members in the above scenario now that you have an evolved understanding?

_____

_____

_____

_____

_____

_____

Now Forgive yourself and have Mercy.

Forgive yourself, because you were not aware of this knowledge and therefore did not fully understand the gravity of being loyal to your desire. Also **appreciate and have mercy** with those you were frustrated with because they were instrumental in reflecting to you your relationship/loyalty to your desires. As a powerful human being it is imperative that you understand the source of all your frustrations. When you are consistently not getting what you truly desire to experience, you become frustrated. Please realize that other people are not the source of your frustration, your disloyalty to your desires is. <u>This is why seeing yourself first in all your relationships is your primary and most important skill to develop in your life.</u> When you truly see yourself you also clearly see what you are desiring.

Now that you are fully aware of your primary responsibility in all of your relationships can you also see why being selfish is so important?

_____yes _____no

"Look at how significant you are. When you are loyal to your desires you are working to produce _Unity_ and Peace within yourself, your family, community and the WORLD. Thank you for contagiously spreading love." Spreadlove Yourself Always

Power Code Ten

Powerful People are United

Have you fully forgiven yourself yet? Are you practicing Mercy?

It is highly important to be forgiving if true unity and peace is to take place. The Latin root for the word unity is unus and initas meaning one, the same and in agreement. Those things we are bitter about and not forgiving of prevent us from working together as one. Forgiveness is critical to everyone's natural way of being, not because it is important that we forgive other people for peace's sake; rather because it affects our own ability to go forward in life. When we do not forgive, it is highlighting a part of our lives that we are not accepting, thus preventing us from fully seeing a reflection of ourselves in others and learning. This uncomfortable experience in your life that you are not accepting is pointing your attention to an aspect of yourself that you are struggling to embrace, for whatever reason. This aspect of yourself that presented it self during the "un-forgivable" experience is what you are having trouble uniting with and it is causing internal conflict. Often times, we do not see this about ourselves because we are so focused on the wrong that the other person did to us and we only see the conflict we are having with others. No peace within equals no peace without.

In order to resolve any external conflict one must always resolve their internal conflict first. As long as there is no internal war going on inside of you, you will always experience instant peace in and outside of you. A key tool to keep in mind that prevents you from becoming distracted is to be conscious of the role your experiences play in your life. Always remember, your experiences in life are never about the other person, they are all about you. You attract your unique experiences based on your unique lesson you need to master at that particular time. Working together as one with others is not a reality if you are not working together as one with your whole self first. In other words, when you are not embracing all of your experiences your integrity is breached and you send out mixed and confusing messages to others. Thus, harmony and unity with others is very difficult in this type of environment.

I can recall a time when I was in my early twenties attending my then boyfriend's family gathering. In the midst of all the fun, one of his aunts, whom he frequently bragged about, mentioned something that exposed my boyfriend. His aunt's conversation totally contradicted something that he told me about her previously. Yes his lie was exposed. It was a simple lie; however, it was a lie nonetheless. My first thought was, how can I trust him if he lies about simple stuff? I could have held this over his head for the duration of our relationship, but I chose to have mercy with him and to move forward. I did not understand why he felt the need to lie, but he did. Besides, how can I judge him when I was just as guilty with little lies too? When I looked in the mirror at myself through him, I saw how telling little lies really did not make any sense. Why would anybody with good sense lie? This was a great lesson for me. Focusing on my lesson allowed me to accept him for who he is and not judge him, besides this was my experience, my lesson to learn. Yes he also had his own lesson to learn too, however, I did not know what his lesson was and it was not my job to know. Understanding that fact, freed me to enjoy our relationship even more so and the many other loving things he brought to the table. I chose to focus on my own growth and it allowed me to grow forward in my life and live it more abundantly exactly the way I desire it to be.

The times when we are not forgiving are directly related to us losing sight of the true nature of living. In our journey on this earth as human beings, we are learning more about ourselves and how to apply our unique purpose more and more effectively daily. Learning is how we maximize our time and fulfill our reason for being on earth. When we do not forgive (unite with ourselves and others), what we are really saying is, "I do not understand how to apply this lesson", and in turn make the judgment that it has no place in our lives. When we think that something we attract has no place in our lives, we do not unite with it. Instead we "throw it away".

When you attract something in your life, how do you determine whether you are going to use it or "throw it away"?

....

_____

_____

_____

Here is one simple way to assist you with measuring whether what you have attracted into your life is for you to use or not.

Everything you attract in your life is specifically designed just for you.

Simple, isn't it? So you do not have to worry or guess about this aspect of your life anymore. Everything you attract in your life from now on, work with it, unite with it, learn from it and see how fast your sense of power, transformation and fulfillment in life manifest. This is the reason why knowing what you desire is so important. When you are aware of your desire it makes the process of embracing and uniting with all of your experiences much easier, this is called oneloving. **Onelove** is seeing and embracing your whole self in all of your experiences. All powerful people use this power code word as well as apply it in everything they do. Will You?

"When you unite with all of your experiences, you unite with everyone around you. Then, and only then, do you truly understand the true nature of your power and its connection to instant Peace."

Onelove Yourself Always

The Power Code Reminders and Quick Steps

Reminders:

Here are a few things to keep in mind as you progress along your self –loyalty journey. Keeping these things in mind will help to keep up your mental body strength so that you will not abandon your progress prematurely.

Reminder one: Involve yourself in things that you enjoy and love doing. One way to guarantee unhappiness and disloyalty is to involve yourself in things that you do not enjoy.

Reminder two: Always have FUN. FUN = Feelings Unfolding Naturally. In order to have real fun you have to be able to relax. And the best way to ensure relaxation for yourself is to be honest. Therefore, having fun requires you to express your real feelings as they naturally arise.

Reminder three: Place yourself in a mental environment that stimulates you, one that allows you to learn more about yourself? Also make it a habit of venturing into new environments; this is very stimulating to your mind. After all, your mind loves being challenged to grow and evolve into a higher level of understanding. Where you put yourself and what opportunities you capitalize on is all up to you.

Reminder four: Whether you know it or not, what you see on the outside of you and the meaning you assign to it reflects your relationship with yourself. You are a part of whatever environment you place yourself in, it is totally dependent on you to evolve it or not. What you put your time, energy and attention on will grow the most. So the fastest way to manifest your desire is to look for it, see it in everything and follow it wherever it takes you.

Quick Steps:

Here are a few quick steps you can use to assist you with continuing the habit of fully expressing the Love 360 language.

- ❖ Step 1 -Appreciate Yourself Always: Whether you or others are aware of it or not, everyone loves you. We just sometimes have a very difficult time expressing it because we are not in acceptance of our whole selves and are not able at that time to express our whole love.
- ❖ Step 2- Get Clear: Before you open your mouth check in with yourself and get clear about what it is you desire so that your words will be in alignment with it.
- ❖ Step 3 - Be Consistent: It is important to demonstrate a consistent message when we say we love one another and we are one. Very often we mention the oneness when we feel like we have fallen short of our goal demonstrating this by including others in our shortcomings. However we quickly develop amnesia of the oneness when we feel we have done something outstanding and are proud of. Be consistently courageous in taking full responsibility for your actions all the time. Look in the mirror at all times, even when you are the only one to blame and do not be afraid to appreciate everyone.
- ❖ Step 4 - Be Self- Determined: make the decision to stay focused on what you desire, especially now that you are acutely aware of how important you and your desires are. You have the power to determine what you will create with your life.
- ❖ Step 5- Enjoy Your Life: You have to Love You in order to enjoy Living Your Life the Way You want to Live it.

The Most Powerful People on this planet are those who have taken full ownership of their life and are creating the life they truly desire to experience.

A P.S. Message about Self Love

When we eat junk, talk about junk, listen to junk or read junk, what is the message we are sending out to the universe? Are we saying that we are utilizing our energy to be a waste receptacle, like the function of a garbage can? Isn't that where we put our junk? If we engage in junk all day what do we call to ourselves? We obviously call more junk, ours and everyone else's. We take on the job of a junk of life waste collector when we are not focused on ourselves and what we desire. Some of us may have collected so much waste that we have upgraded our job and moved from garbage cans to dumpsters and from dumpsters to waste landfills. Gossip, blaming, complaining, junk, mess, garbage, poor performance, poverty, depression, disease, anger, relationship drama and un-forgiveness are all what we at the Real Help Center call Human Relationship Waste (HRW). Regain your Power by utilizing the language of the Most Powerful People on the Planet: Love 360!

<u>Love 360 and Experience the love that everyone has for you.</u>

May you always make space in your life for love.

Yours Truly,
Stephanie Jupiter

A word from my mother the encourager:

Shalom Angels. Every day as much as possible smile it opens the heart chakra. Organize, prioritize, and obey your divine orders for your day and you will see more of your prosperity and greatness!!!!!
Complete at least one divine task daily to be encouraged.

Sincerely,
Mother Divine Seraphim Peg

Love 360 Vocabulary Glossary

LOVE 360 is a primordial Sanskrit language, it is the original language of the heart. It is the language of all human beings, it is irrespective of race, gender, age or social status. It has no boundaries because it is not limited by words and/ or symbols. The basic introduction to this language uses words in order to allow people to have a common understanding since we are more accustomed to communicating with each other through words and symbols. However once you tap into the basic understanding of the nature of the language you will begin to harmoniously tap into the rhythm of the language. Once you are in rhythm with the language you will be able to express it with very little effort.

Reloving: recycling the unconditional love the universe has for you. Pg. 14

Possibilities: an unlimited amount of abilities existing within the universe designed to create opportunities for you to get all of your desires met in any way imaginable. Pg. 18

Patience: concentrating on your abilities long enough, giving them time to mature and facilitate you in getting precisely what you desire. Pg. 22

Preloving: when you are being patient. Pg. 22

Inlove: acknowledging your feelings and become one with them. Pg. 25

Honesty: honoring your feelings and being truthful about your understanding of them. Honesty is designed to emphasize the particular lesson you are engaged in at any given time. Pg. 30

Fulloving: the act of unconditionally taking total ownership for every part of your life. pg. 36

Truloving: responsibly taking care of your spirit, mind and body's daily nutritional requirements. Pg. 40

Allearsloving: undividedly paying attention to your wisdom from within. Pg. 44

Openloving: trusting the fact that everything is working in your favor to assist you with your growth and fulfillment all the time. pg 50

Godloving: understanding and trusting that you always attract to yourself what you are truly desiring. Pg. 56

Spreadloving: being one with your desires and inspiring others to be one with theirs too. Pg. 60

Onelove: seeing and embracing your whole self in all of your experiences. Pg. 67

End of Course Exam

Answer these five questions:

1. What is your personal formula for happiness?

   _____

2. Who you are is who you want to be? _____yes _____no

3. What is one definite cure for SADD and A.I.V. (Artificial Intelligence Virus)?

   _____

4. What is the Self Love Law?

   _____

   _____

5. What is your unique purpose?

   _____

   _____

If you would like to receive a certificate for completing this course please email your responses to:

Stephanie@relationshipfitnesscenter.com or soluniversity@ therealhelp.com

Or physically mail to:
Science of Life University
P.O. Box 421103
Houston, Texas 77242

Make sure to include the name you would like to appear on your Certificate. Also provide your contact information including an email address and telephone number. Thank you.

Contact information:
Stephanie Jupiter
P.O. Box 421103
Houston, Texas 77242
stephanie@relationshipfitnesscenter.com or
soluniversity@therealhelp.com